a ^smart girl's guide to
parties

how to be a great guest,
be a happy hostess,
and have fun at
any kind of party

by Apryl Lundsten
illustrated by Angela Martini

★ American Girl®

Questions or comments? Call 1-800-845-0005,
visit our Web site at **americangirl.com**, or write to Customer Service,
American Girl, 8400 Fairway Place, Middleton, WI 53562.

Printed in China
10 11 12 13 14 LEO 10 9 8 7 6 5 4 3 2 1

Editorial Development: Carrie Anton
Art Direction and Design: Cesca Piuma, Chris David
Production: Tami Kepler, Judith Lary, Sarah Boecher, Jeannette Bailey
Illustrations: Angela Martini

Dear Reader,

Parties are a great way to celebrate important occasions, such as birthdays, anniversaries, and graduations—but they're also good for recognizing smaller wins in life such as acing that math test you studied so hard for or performing your first dance recital in front of a huge crowd.

In this book, you'll find all kinds of party-going and party-throwing tips so that you can have the best time possible at any party, whether you're a guest or the hostess. You'll also learn the answers to such party questions as:

- How can I meet people at a party where I know only the hostess?

- What happens if I get homesick at a slumber party?

- How do I decide who to invite to my birthday party?

- What do I say to a guest who gave me a gift I don't like?

You'll hear from girls just like you about how they handled their own party predicaments. And you'll also get the scoop on what to do if you're not invited to a party, what to expect at boy-girl parties, suggestions for do-it-yourself gifts, and how to write the perfect thank-you note.

So turn the page and get ready to party!

Your friends at American Girl

contents

Guest Guide

This section is your go-to guide for everything you need to know about being the perfect partygoer. You'll find tips about how to RSVP (yes, we'll tell you what it means!) and what to do if you get invited to a party but your best friend doesn't. Plus, there's a quiz to help you figure out what kind of party guest you are, ideas for making conversation with someone you just met, and advice on how to deal with all kinds of "oops!" party moments.

you're invited

your guide to being a great guest

on the guest list

Yay! You've been invited to a party! Excited? You should be! But before the fun can begin, there's something all guests must do: **RSVP ASAP!**

RSVP is French for "répondez s'il vous plaît" (pronounced rey-pawn-dey seel voo pleh), which means "please reply." It's important to respond to an invitation as soon as possible to let the hostess know whether or not you can attend her party.

Check the "respond by" date on the invitation—it might say something such as "RSVP by March 15" or "Please respond by November 10."

There will usually be a phone number for you to call, an e-mail address to write to, or a card to mail back. It's best to respond right away. That way you won't forget and leave the hostess hanging, and right from the start you'll be on your way to being a great guest.

Can't go

If you already know you can't go to the party, let the hostess know as soon as you can. Tell her how happy you were to get the invitation and how bummed you are that you have to miss her party.

Last minute can't make it

Sometimes things come up that can't be avoided. You might get the flu or have to visit sick Uncle Ted in the hospital. Canceling at the last minute can be really disappointing—for you *and* the hostess. Give the hostess a call right away. Let her or her parents know you can't come and be sure to tell them why.

A phone call is best so that you can actually speak to a person. If you send an e-mail, she might not get it until the party is over and worry about where you are.

left out

I know someone who invited every girl in my class but me to her party. I thought we were friends. What did I do wrong?

Getting left out happens to all of us at some point. It's no fun, but it may have nothing to do with you personally. Maybe there was a limit to how many people could be invited, or the hostess's parents made the final decisions on the guest list. Either way, accept the situation as it is, and don't let it sour your friendship.

On the day of the party, avoid moping around the house by having something fun planned—start a craft project, create a playlist of your favorite songs, get lost in a great book, or plan a sleepover with another friend who was not invited.

I got invited to a party but my best friend didn't. Now I'm afraid to tell her.

Even if you're trying to spare your friend's feelings, you should be honest about receiving an invitation. Keeping a secret can lead to feelings of hurt and betrayal, which can poison a friendship. Suggest doing something together on a different day. And, unless she asks, don't talk too much about the party afterward.

know before you go

No two parties are exactly the same, but with the exception of sleepovers, most parties follow similar schedules.

After guests arrive, the hostess will introduce everyone and leave time for chatting. Sometimes a light snack, such as chips and soda, will be served while guests get to know each other better.

Then there's often some sort of activity, such as playing games or sports, swimming, dancing, or doing something that matches the party's theme.

Following the activity, it's time to eat—usually pizza, burgers, or cake is served.

If it's a birthday party, opening presents might follow the meal.

After that, it's usually time to go.

Guests are usually friends and family members of the hostess. Some guests may know each other from school, but there may be other guests who don't, such as the hostess's cousin or girls from her ballet class.

The hostess's mom and dad, or other adult, will chaperone the party. They're there to make sure the party goes smoothly.

The one thing you can count on is that the hostess wants all her guests to have a good time.

Party pro

Just like getting good at a sport or musical instrument, being comfortable in new situations takes practice. Follow these tips to become a party pro.

"Be me"

Tell yourself this simple statement—and practice it regularly! *Being myself means I'm:*

- *confident;*

- *happy with who I am; and*

- *OK knowing I'm not always going to be perfect.* (Who's perfect, anyway? Nobody!)

Strength in numbers

If your friends are also invited to the party, go together. That way you have a built-in support group to talk to, dance with, and depend on. Having friends around can help you relax.

What to bring

- Gifts: If it's a birthday party, try to ask the hostess questions that will give you clues about what gift she would like.

- Food: Should you bring any snacks or drinks?

- Other items: Is there anything you need to bring, such as skates, music, or a sleeping bag?

Greeting parents

When meeting your hostess's parents, be polite and pleasant.
Introduce yourself.

Hi, Mr. and Mrs. Jackson!
I'm Kimberly.

When you leave the party, be sure to say "good-bye" to the
hostess's parents and thank them for inviting you.

Helping hand
If you're one of the first guests to arrive, find out if there's anything you can do to help the hostess get ready for the party. Being helpful can ease you into a social situation and give you something to do.

Get real
Sure, you want to be charming and entertaining and make a lasting impression on everyone at the party, but be realistic. The most important thing is to be yourself and have fun. Worrying about doing and saying everything perfectly isn't necessary and doesn't help.

Keep it in perspective
Parties can seem really, really important—and they are, to a point. But your entire life does not depend on what happens at one party. Even if you trip over your own feet in front of everyone, or blurt out something you wish you hadn't said, don't worry about it too much. Everyone has done something embarrassing at one point or another.

getting dressed

What you wear to a party depends on a few things:

• how fancy the party is
• what you'll be doing at the party
• the season or weather

Here are some party outfit options to consider:

Casual party
• jeans and a tee
• shorts and a tank top
• skirt and a hoodie
• sundress

**Dinner party with your parents,
or with your friend and her parents**
• dress pants and a blouse
• skirt and sweater
• dressy jacket and skirt
• sweater dress with leggings

**Wedding reception or other
formal party**
• fancy dress
• skirt and blouse
• black dress and a dressy cardigan

Make sure that whatever you wear fits you well and is comfortable. There's no reason to wear an outfit—no matter how cute it is—that has you squirming the whole time.

Activewear

Think about what you're going to be doing at the party. Are you spending the night? Going on a hayride? Cooking? Swimming? Dancing? Wear—or pack—something that's appropriate for the party's activities. If you don't know what you'll be doing, ask ahead!

Ready to wear

Getting ready at the last minute can be really stressful. Choose your outfit ahead of time. Be sure it's clean. Lay it out or keep all the pieces together, hanging separately from the rest of your clothes.

what kind of guest are you?

1. You see a party as:

   a. a place to show off your dance moves.

   b. just another fun way to hang out with your friends.

   c. ack—nerve-wracking!

2. What kind of pajamas would you wear at a slumber party?

   a. a brand-new pair of trendy PJs that you bought just for the party

   b. whatever is clean in your dresser

   c. one of your dad's big, long comfy T-shirts, which reminds you of home

3. How many guests do you think are needed to make a good party?

   a. a huge group with lots of people

   b. a medium-sized group that mixes people who both know and don't know each other

   c. a small group of your closest friends

4. Your favorite party activities are:

   a. dancing, playing charades, and singing karaoke.

   b. games where you get to know your friends better or scavenger hunts where you're all working together as a team.

   c. watching movies and doing crafts.

5. You're at a party where you only know the hostess. You:

a. approach a group and tell them your name and what school you go to.

b. introduce yourself to a couple of other girls who seem to be on their own, too.

c. spot a magazine on the coffee table and bury yourself in one of the articles.

6. If there's a party, you're usually the one:

a. hosting it.

b. talking with as many of the guests as possible.

c. worrying about what to say, what to wear, and how to act.

Answers

Center of Attention

If you chose **mostly a's,** you're the life of the party! Outgoing, friendly, and brimming with confidence, you like it when all eyes (and ears) are on you. Just don't become an attention hog. Remember, you're not the only one at the party! Use your positive, upbeat energy to encourage shy guests to open up.

Miss Mixer

If you chose **mostly b's,** you love going to parties to hang out with your friends. You tend to get along with lots of different kinds of people and can strike up a conversation with just about everyone. Use your socializing talent to bring people together who wouldn't normally be friends.

Wallflower

If you chose **mostly c's,** you're probably most comfortable in small groups of people you know well. While that's great for girl bonding, it's good to step out of your comfort zone from time to time. Try introducing yourself to someone else who tends to be on the shy side—you might make a great new pal! Or call on your friends to help you join in on a group activity so that you have a familar face by your side.

don't know anyone? don't worry!

What do you do if you walk into a party where you don't know *any* of the guests? It might seem scary, but think about it as a great chance to make new friends.

Make the first move
Go up to a group of people and introduce yourself. Ask a question to get a conversation started.

"Hi, I'm Alice. I'm Emma's friend from camp. How do you know Emma?"

Count on a friend
Ask the hostess to introduce you to someone. Or, if the hostess is talking to someone you don't know and you want to meet that person, ask if you can join their conversation.

At your service
If you're going up for seconds or getting up to grab an extra napkin, offer to get something for another guest. She will appreciate the nice gesture, and it gives you something to talk about.

Do you like pepperoni or mushroom?

conversation starters

Want to talk but don't know what to say? Try these talking tips to help get you chatting.

Conversation starters

Talk about something that affects both of you at the moment. For example, "I've never heard this song before. Do you know who sings it?"

Compliments

Compliments can go a long way. If you like another guest's sweater or haircut, let her know. And if someone compliments you, use it to kick off a conversation. "Thanks! I was nervous about getting a short style, but it's great for me because I play soccer. Do *you* play any sports?"

Things in common

If the guest is in one of your classes, talk about the teacher, what unit you're on, or your last pop quiz. "I really like our science class, because our teacher does the best projects."

Questions

Asking questions is a great way to get people to open up to you.

- What songs are on your MP3 player?
- What books have you read recently?
- What kind of hobbies do you have?

Listen up

The best conversationalist isn't always the person who talks the most. Show interest in the person you're talking to by asking questions and focusing on what she's saying instead of just waiting to talk again. "Wow, you do karate? I've never tried it. How did you get started with that?"

be a great guest

Give the hostess the gift of being a good guest. Even if it means playing a game you don't like or doing an activity you've never tried, look on the bright side:

- You're spending time with your friends.
- You're trying different things.
- You're learning how to be patient, respectful, and generous.

It's not about you

No one can have her way all the time. A party—especially a birthday party—is for the girl hosting it. Guests are there to celebrate her. That means doing what she wants to do (unless it's not safe, of course), even if it's watching *her* favorite movie for the fifth time!

Be flexible

Most things in life don't turn out exactly the way we think they will, and parties are no exception. You might be planning on going to a pool party, but it ends up pouring rain on party day. Be willing to go with the flow and handle any change of plans that might come up during the party. Not only will you make things easier for the hostess by being flexible, but a better attitude will help you have a better time.

House rules

Every house has rules, and when you're at a friend's house, you have to follow her family's rules. But some rules should go without saying:

• Be polite and courteous.

• Don't go through other people's belongings, such as in closets, drawers, or medicine cabinets.

• Use appropriate language.

• Ask permission before you use the phone, stereo, television, or computer or get food or beverages from the refrigerator.

• Stay at the party—don't leave without an adult's permission.

• Clean up after yourself.

Dealing with rule breakers

What should you do if you're at a party where girls are breaking the rules? Maybe they're acting wild, using the phone to make prank calls, or watching a movie they're not supposed to watch. Whatever is happening, the situation is tricky, and it can be difficult to know what to do—especially if most or all of the girls are going along with the mischief, or if it's the hostess who's causing the trouble.

• Don't go along with the rule breakers. Joining in isn't going to make the troublemaking right.

• Try to change the focus. Suggest a different activity you know in a lighthearted and casual way: "Who wants to play a game instead?" If they all say no, consider doing something on your own such as reading a magazine or listening to music.

• Speak up. Let them know you're not comfortable with what's going on.

• If the others are doing something dangerous, tell an adult. It's only tattling if you're trying to get someone *into* trouble instead of *out of* trouble.

Girl gab

Parties are great for gabbing, but when the talk is about people not at the party, that's gossiping. We've all been in situations where someone has made comments that put another person down. It's hard to stop people from saying mean things about others, but you can try, by bringing up the positive things about that person or simply changing the subject. It's OK to say:

I don't want to talk about Anna. She's my friend, just like you. I wouldn't let other people talk about you that way.

If you and the other partygoers share secrets about yourselves, watch what you share. If you don't want anyone outside the party to ever know, it's best to just keep your lips sealed.

Say what?

Speaking up and joining the conversation is important, but avoid being the attention hog. You should feel comfortable offering your opinions, telling jokes and stories, and revealing your feelings. Just try not to take over the conversation. Let other people talk, and don't steal away attention from the hostess.

Remember that a nice compliment goes a long way. Tell some fun and flattering stories about the hostess, such as how she won the school spelling bee or scored the final point in basketball. Use your gift for gab to celebrate your hostess, which at the same time allows you to still be your outgoing, talkative self.

Keep in mind how loudly you're talking or laughing. Turn the volume down a notch. You don't have to shout or scream to be heard.

party cliques

Cliques (pronounced "clicks") are groups of people who are tight-knit and seem closed off from everyone but themselves. If you go to a party where many of the guests are part of a clique, it might be hard to be a great guest if you feel left out of conversations or activities. Here are some tips about how to deal with cliques:

- Don't let a clique's bad attitude affect you. It's usually not really about you, but about them feeling powerful and better than you.

- Don't put on an act to try to impress anyone. There's no need to pretend to be something you're not or go along with the crowd's opinion if you really disagree.

- Pal up with other guests at the party who aren't part of the clique. If you don't know them, introduce yourself.

- Don't keep to yourself or say nothing at all just because you're worried what the girls in the clique might think of you. It's best to be yourself.

If you're the only one at the party who isn't part of the clique and are stuck standing alone, offer to help out the hostess or her parents with anything that needs to be done for the party. Lending a hand will keep you busy and make you feel useful.

oops!

Oh, no! You dropped salsa down the front of your sweater. Comfort yourself by keeping in mind that we're all human and "oops" moments happen to everyone.

Oops: You blurted out something you wished you hadn't said.
Quick fix: Sometimes our mouths seem to move without checking with our brains first. Just apologize. "I can't believe I just said that! I'm really sorry!"

Oops: You spilled something all over the chair or on another guest.
Quick fix: For the furniture, immediately tell the hostess's parents. Don't try to clean up the mess yourself (the stain may require a special cleaning solution), and don't try to pretend it didn't happen by covering it up with a napkin. If you spill on someone else, apologize and get a napkin or paper towel right away.

Oops: You tripped in front of everyone and fell flat on your face.
Quick fix: As long as you're not badly hurt, make a joke of your mistake. Jump up and dust yourself off, take a bow, pretend you're winning an Olympic medal, or finish the "stunt" with a twirl. Or simply say, "I meant to do that!" Then laugh it off.

Oops: You forgot someone's name or called her by the wrong name.
Quick fix: It's really easy to get someone's name wrong or forget her name altogether. Apologize for getting it wrong and repeat it back to yourself to help you remember for next time. If you just can't remember the person's name, it's OK to say, "I'm sorry, I forgot your name. What is it again?"

Oops: The parents talked to you about being too loud.
Quick fix: Apologize and promise you'll keep it down—and then make sure you keep your promise. If they have to keep coming in to tell you to be quiet, you might not be asked to come over again.

Oops: You tore the backside of your pants.
Quick fix: If you are at a party such as a sleepover and brought a change of clothes, this would be a good time to put them on so you don't make the damage any worse. If you didn't bring another outfit, get your sweatshirt (or ask to borrow a friend's) and tie it around your waist.

Oops: Your stomach growled really loud.
Quick fix: Our bodies do crazy things and sometimes make some pretty outrageous noises. You could say "Excuse me!" to be polite, or try to laugh it off by making a joke. "Who knew there was a monster inside me!"

Oops: You took too much food and can't finish what's on your plate.
Quick fix: It's simple enough to say, "Oops! I took too many chips. Does anyone want a few?"

Oops: You accidentally broke something at the party.
Quick fix: Take responsibility for the mishap and tell the hostess's parents right away. The sooner you let them know, the more chance there might be that the item can be fixed. For things that can be replaced, you may want to offer to replace the item. Be sure to tell your parents what happened so that they can talk with the hostess's parents.

Saying you're sorry

Many "oops" moments can be cleared up with an apology. Follow these tips when the time comes to say you're sorry:
- Take responsibility for what you did.
- Really mean what you say.
- Apologize in front of other people.
- Don't use excuses.

Instead of:

It wasn't my fault. Everyone was roughhousing.

say,

I'm really sorry I broke your mug, Mr. Ruiz. I will try to be more careful.

Instead of:

The DVD was already broken before I ever touched it.

say,

Mrs. Stephens, I'm so sorry for breaking your DVD. Please let me and my parents know if you'd like us to pay for a new one.

If you do break something, it's best to follow up with a written apology to the hostess's parents.

Dear Mr. and Mrs. Hamilton,

I wanted to apologize again for breaking the pitcher. It really was an accident, but I should've been more careful. I'm going to use my allowance to buy you a new one.

Aside from the mistake, I really had a nice time at Gabby's slumber party. I hope to have her over for a sleepover of my own soon.

Sorry again. I hope you can forgive me!

Sincerely,
Lauren Moore

party smarts

everything you need to know about going to all kinds of parties

a sleepover story

The guests are dropped off.

Time to eat!

Activity time!

Watching a movie

Talking, laughing, sharing, and bonding

Getting ready for bed

The next morning

Time to go home

what to pack

Checklist

	✓
sleeping bag	✓
pillow	✓
pajamas	✓
toothbrush, toothpaste, floss	✓
hairbrush	✓
change of clothes for the next day	✓
gift, if it's a birthday party	✓

Sleeping bag pal

If you want, you can also bring a favorite blanket or stuffed animal. It's natural to get homesick even if you're only spending one night away from your own bed. Having something familiar along can help you feel more comfortable.

Special extras

Depending on what activities are planned for the party, you may need to bring additional equipment, clothes, or gear. Find out from the hostess if you need to bring anything else.

Changing

If you can't have a room to yourself to change, here's a way to slip into your PJs without totally undressing.

- Pull your arms in through your sleeves.

- While still in your T-shirt, put on your PJ top and button it up.

- Slip off your T-shirt over your head through the neck of the PJs. Remove your jeans and slip on your PJ bottoms.

do's and don'ts

Snack time

Dinner was done an hour ago, but you're hungry again. You'd like to go to the kitchen for a snack but aren't sure if it's OK.

Don't: Act as if there are no rules. It might be fine to eat anytime at home, but your hostess might not be allowed between-meal snacks.

Do: Ask the hostess and her parents if it's OK to have a snack and where you can eat it.

Loudmouth

You're trying to sleep, but a couple of girls are keeping you awake with their loud chatter.

Don't: Be bossy or angry about it. There's no reason to hiss a nasty "Shh!" or tell them to "shut up!" Being rude might encourage them to be rude, too, and cause them to get even louder.

Do: Ask them politely to turn down the volume a notch.

Teasing

You and your friend have a certain connection—you finish each other's sentences, you know all of each other's deepest secrets, and the two of you can joke with each other as if you were sisters. But poking fun at other people might not get the same reaction.

Don't: Get too sarcastic, personal, or mean when you tell stories. It's best not to tease each other—even playfully.

Do: Tell funny stories everyone will enjoy, and trade jokes.

Playing pranks

You've probably heard about pranks being pulled at slumber parties, such as prank phone calls or practical jokes played on the first girl who falls asleep.

Don't: Be the joker—especially if you know that some of the other girls aren't comfortable with pranks. Never pull a prank on someone while she's sleeping and don't ever pull pranks that are humiliating or could be dangerous.

Do: Talk to the other girls before the party starts about skipping the pranks. It's likely that there are other girls who feel just like you do. Find a friend at the party who feels the same way, and talk to the rest of the group together about making the party a no-prank zone.

If you overhear someone talking about pulling a prank that could hurt someone, be sure to let an adult at the party know.

bedtime blues

For lots of girls, the *slumber* part of a slumber party can be tough. It's hard to fall asleep when you're missing home or don't feel good. Keep reading to find out about real girls—just like you—who get bedtime blues.

I'm going for a sleepover at my friend's house, but I get homesick really bad. Should I go or just stay home?

Don't miss out on the fun! Just be prepared. Pack something familiar—your favorite blanket, pillow, or stuffed animal—to help you feel more at home when you go to bed. Let your friend and her parents know you tend to get homesick—that way they'll already know and will be able to be there for you. If you're really missing home, phone Mom and Dad. Sometimes just a quick "hello" will have you feeling better fast.

I get stomach aches a lot. My friend just invited me to her slumber party. I want to go, but what should I do if my stomach starts to hurt at her house?

Don't panic! Everyone gets tummy aches. Whether your stomach is upset from eating too many chips or you're coming down with the flu, the best thing to do is tell the hostess's parents. They can give you something to help your stomach and will be able to determine if you need to go home.

I can't sleep without listening to classical music. My friends don't like it and I don't want to be rude, but without music I can't sleep the rest of the night! What should I do?

If you can, bring an MP3 player and headphones. That way you can still listen to music, but you won't disturb anyone. If you don't have an MP3 player and can't borrow one, try this relaxation technique: Close your eyes and think of a peaceful place, such as the beach. Breathe slowly and imagine the sun on your body, your toes in the sand, and the sound of the ocean.

I'm afraid of the dark. I don't want my friends to make fun of me. What should I do?

Don't be afraid to tell your friends about your fear. Chances are, one of them might be scared, too. Ask the hostess if she can turn on a nightlight—that way it won't be totally dark, but it won't be too light to sleep.

During my sleepover, my best friend started crying because she was homesick. I didn't know what to do!

This can be really hard because you want your friend to feel comfortable—and spend the night again! Let her know you understand how she feels and that you're there to talk if she needs to. Maybe go with her to make a phone call to her parents or offer a favorite stuffed animal that helps you feel less homesick.

dinner parties

Going to parties with Mom, Dad, and their friends can be a lot of fun. Sure, they're adults, but if you know what to do, you'll have a great time—and polish your party skills!

Introductions
Always speak to adults using "Mr.," "Mrs.," or "Ms." unless you've been told it's OK to call them by their first names or nicknames.

Hang it up
Ask the hostess where she'd like you to place your coat; don't just toss it on a chair or dump it in a pile on the floor. Offer to take Mom's and Dad's coats, too.

Help out
Ask the hosts if they need any help. Offer to gather coats and purses, hand out napkins, or pass out appetizers. This not only shows how helpful and polite you are, it also gives you something to do (rather than sitting around wishing you were doing something else).

The only non-adult at the party
Find out from your parents if you're going to be the only person your age at the party. If so, ask if you can bring a book, your MP3 player, or a DVD to watch. You can also have your parents ask if it would be OK for you to watch TV there. Just be sure to join the party when you're asked to and answer any questions that are directed to you. It's rude to stay focused on your book or movie when someone is trying to speak to you.

gabbing with grown-ups

Talking to adults can seem intimidating, but remember that you've already had some practice talking with your parents, teachers, and aunts and uncles. If you want to be more comfortable gabbing with grown-ups, keep these things in mind.

Talking trash

Try not to, like, um, totally fill your sentences with garbage words that, like, um, totally don't mean anything, you know? Talk to grown-ups the same way you'd talk to teachers or other adults at school—in full sentences and with respect.

Icebreakers

It can be hard to start a conversation with an adult—especially if you're not used to doing it. Most of the time, the adult will lead the conversation, but that doesn't mean you have to leave it all up to him or her. There are lots of things to talk about:

- the meal you're eating
- the music being played
- subjects you're studying in school
- books you've read
- movies you've seen
- your favorite sports or favorite sports teams

Avoid

- personal information about your family
- critical comments about anyone

How was your day, Mrs. Mott?

Questions

It's OK to ask adults questions—just don't ask questions that are too nosy.

Don't ask: "I heard you lost your job, Mr. Young. How did that happen?"

Ask: "How are you, Mr. Young?"

Other questions to steer clear of are ones that have to do with money, politics, religion, or personal appearance. For example, you should never ask anyone how much something cost, how old an adult is, or how much a person weighs.

Don't ask:

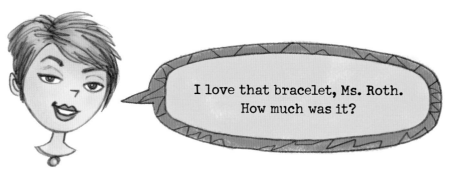

I love that bracelet, Ms. Roth. How much was it?

Ask:

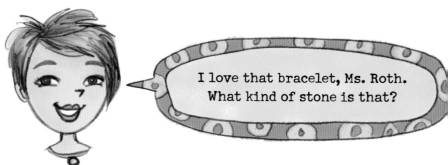

I love that bracelet, Ms. Roth. What kind of stone is that?

Whenever I go to parties with grown-ups, I get nervous. Can't I just pretend they aren't there?

Ignoring them isn't going to help and is just going to make you seem rude. You don't have to be Miss Charm. A simple "Hello, Mr. Roberts. Nice to see you again," is fine. And remember to say "please," "thank you," and "excuse me."

What should I say to comments such as, "Wow, you've really grown?"

Sometimes adults want to talk to kids but don't know what to say. So they say generic things, such as "My, you've grown up." Try responding with something more personal about yourself, such as "I'm in fourth grade now. I don't know if my mom told you, but I take ballet and play piano." Tell them what moves you've learned in dance class or what song you're practicing. This should open the door for them to ask you more questions about what you're doing. You could also try asking them if they know your favorite band, book, movie, TV show, sports team, or Web site. It's possible they will—or that they'll want to know more.

Can I go up to a group of grown-ups and join their conversation?

If the adults are laughing and talking casually, sure! Do it just like you would with people your own age. Wait for a break in the conversation and say, "Excuse me, do you mind if I join your conversation?" If there are people in the group you don't know, introduce yourself and find out their names.

What do I do if one of my mom's friends asks me something that's too personal—either about me or our family?

You don't have to answer! Tell her, "I'm sorry, but that's private." And then change the subject by asking her something about Sunday's big game or the latest movie she's seen.

food for thought

Do your manners shine, or do they need polish? Take this quiz to find

1. Dinner is served and you get your plate first. It smells great, and you can hardly wait to dig in.

   a. You dig in! After all, you don't want the food to get cold.

   b. You wait until everybody else has been served and the hostess takes a bite before you dig in.

   c. You take little nibbles when you think nobody is looking.

2. Oh, no! There's a UFO on your plate—an Unidentified Food Object.

   a. You say, "I'm not eating that."

   b. You take a tiny taste to see if you like it.

   c. You hide it under some mashed potatoes.

3. Leave it to Aunt Beth to be fancy. There are three forks at your place. Three?!! Which one should you use first?

   a. Watch and see which one the hostess uses, and use the same.

   b. Ask. There's no such thing as a dumb question, right?

   c. Start with the outside one first.

4. You wanted to sit next to your cousin Wendy. Instead, you're sitting by Granny Harris. "Hello, sweet pea," she says. "How's school?"

   a. "Fine," you say, and look around to see where Wendy's sitting.

   b. You pretend you didn't hear her and make an igloo out of your mashed potatoes.

   c. You tell Granny all about your art project. Then you ask her about her new glasses.

5. From across the table, your dad says, "Please pass the peas." They're sitting in front of you.

   a. You pass the peas to the right.

   b. You pass the peas to the left.

   c. You scoop up some peas and say, "Please pass your plate, Dad."

6. Uncle Andrew is telling you a long story when you realize you really, really have to go to the bathroom.

   a. You say, "Was that a knock at the door?" and run from the table.

   b. You sit there until you think you're going to explode, because it's rude to interrupt.

   c. You say, "Excuse me, Uncle Andrew." Then you ask the hostess, "May I be excused for a moment, please?"

7. Halfway through the meal you notice that Aunt Shannon has a glob of cranberry stuck in her teeth.

   a. You catch her eye and make a little motion with your hand by your mouth to let her know.

   b. You say, "Hey, Shannon. You've got something stuck in your teeth!"

   c. You do nothing. You don't want to embarrass her!

Answers

1. The answer is b. It's not polite to eat in front of somebody who doesn't have any food. Why? Because watching you eat makes that person hungrier. The hostess is in charge of making sure everybody is served. Then she'll begin eating—and so can you.

2. The answer is b. If somebody puts something new on your plate, you should give it a try. Hiding it fools no one, and telling the cook you don't like the looks of it is just rude.

3. The answers are a, b, and c. They're all right! Whenever you aren't sure what to do, you can ask someone or just wait and see what the hostess does. But there is also a nifty secret to every fancy place setting: the silverware for the food that's served first is placed farthest from the plate.

4. The answer is c. Conversation is the most important part of the meal, so don't clam up just because you're not sitting next to your favorite relative. Be friendly! Ask some questions. You and Granny will never get to know each other if you don't give good conversation a chance.

5. The answer is a. Pass food, not plates. Food is passed to the right. If you send something the wrong way, two platters are going to end up nose to nose. If it's a big dish, help the next person by holding it while she serves herself.

6. The answer is c. There are times it's OK to interrupt an adult if you do so nicely, and this is one of those times. Most adults will understand what you're thinking, and you can slip away without any fuss.

7. The answer is a. If you tell the whole table that Shannon's got a glob in her teeth, she will be embarrassed. But letting her go through the whole meal with that glob will embarrass her more. The kindest thing is to let her know in a private way what you noticed.

formal events

Attending your best friend's bowling birthday party is very different from attending your aunt's wedding. Formal parties often require getting dressed up and being on your best behavior. Weddings are one example of a formal event, but there are others, too.

Christenings and baptisms are religious celebrations. They usually take place in a church with a reception after the service.

Bar mitzvahs and bat mitzvahs are Jewish coming-of-age ceremonies that usually take place at age 13 for boys and age 12 for girls. The service takes place in a temple and includes a reading from the Torah in Hebrew. After the service, there is usually a boy-girl party for friends and family with a DJ, dancing, and food.

A quinceañera (pronounced kin-say-NYE-ra) is a Latin-American celebration of a girl's 15th birthday. She dresses up in a white ball gown, almost like a wedding dress, and sometimes goes to a special Mass at church. She's usually attended by *damas* (like bridesmaids) and *chambelanes* (the damas' male escorts) and escorted by a "man of honor." After Mass, there's usually a big party at a ballroom with lots of food and dancing. It's traditional for the quinceañera and her attendants to perform a waltz for the guests. After her party, the quinceañera is considered to be a young woman.

A cotillion (pronounced ko-TIL-yen) is a debutante, or "coming out," ball. In the past, they were held to introduce young women to society. Today, they're more likely to be fancy-dress parties where guests enjoy a formal dinner and learn ballroom dancing and table manners.

Beat boredom

Not all formal parties are as fun as you might think they'd be. Banish boredom with these simple games.

Color game: Count the number of people wearing blue. Then count how many are wearing red, yellow, green, black, pink, and white. What is the most popular color at the party?

Reporter for a day: Pretend you're a journalist, and think of how you would report the story of the event. Keep in mind who the story is about (Sammy Simon), what the story is (Sammy is celebrating her bat mitzvah), when it's taking place (Saturday, June 10), where it's taking place (Temple Beth Hillel), why the event is happening (she turned 12), and how it is celebrated (a big party).

Word games: Before you go to the event, come up with a "word of the day," like "marriage" or "celebration." Count how many times the word is used during the event or listen to the last word of every sentence and think of a word that rhymes with it. See how fast you can do it!

Memory game: Without staring, study the person sitting in front of you for five seconds. What color is her hair? Her outfit? Is she wearing jewelry? Is her hair short or long? Look away and try to remember everything you can. Check back to see if there's anything you forgot.

Celebrity sighting: Most people look a little like someone famous. Scan the crowd for celebrity look-alikes. Do you see someone who looks like the president? Your favorite actress? A popular singer?

giving gifts

ideas for nifty and thrifty gifts

nifty gifts

Gifts show our friends and family we care about them. You're supposed to bring gifts to certain events, such as birthday parties, graduations, bridal and baby showers, weddings, and holiday parties.

Some people also bring a "hostess gift" to a party. This is a small token to show appreciation to a person for throwing a get-together.

The right present

Think about the person you're getting the gift for. What does she like to do?

Do you know her favorite...

movie?

singer?

book?

dessert?

Good gifts tell your friend how much you she means to you. So try to pick out presents that are meaningful to her or that say how special your friendship is. Don't get her the latest CD from *your* favorite band, unless you're really, *really* sure that she would love it, too!

More gift ideas
Still stumped about what to get? Here are more ideas.

For the friend who loves to **swim:**
- a personalized beach bag
- flip-flops in her favorite color
- a pretty swimsuit cover-up

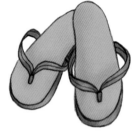

For the friend who loves to **cook:**
- a cupcake cookbook and paper baking cups decorated with cute patterns
- a personalized apron
- an herb-garden kit

For the friend who **cares about the environment:**
- anything handmade
- a wallet or tote bag made from recycled materials
- a grow-your-own-tree kit

For the friend who is **artistic:**
- a scrapbook kit
- a craft bin filled with colorful beads
- colored pencils in a pretty case and an artist sketchpad

For the friend who loves **gadgets:**
- cute earbud covers
- a jump drive in a fun shape
- rhinestone decals and carrying case for her gadget

For the friend who loves **fashion:**
- a bold-patterned tote bag
- fabric patches and embellishments to add to clothing
- a matching set of earrings and necklace

Go-to gifts

If you just don't have a clue about what to get, here are some ideas that can work for all kinds of people:

- a framed picture of you and your friend

- room accessories, such as cute pillows for her bed or a matching desk set

- a relaxation set that includes a yoga mat and yoga book or DVD

- a "just for fun" kit filled with a new card game, joke book, and silly stuffed animal

- cold-weather gear, such as a matching hat, scarf, and fingerless gloves

thrifty gifts

Thoughtful gifts don't have to cost a lot or come from a mall.

Inexpensive options

The perfect dish: Ask the friends of the birthday girl to give you their favorite recipes (that they either like to make or just like to eat). Gather all of the recipes together in a special recipe book.

Movies and a snack: Microwave flavored popcorn and put it in a pretty bowl. Wrap the bowl in a clear gift bag and attach coupons for movie rentals to the outside bow.

Desk set: Fill a cute mug with different-colored pens and pencils. Package them with different kinds of stationery and writing paper.

Locker decor: Cut a piece of wrapping paper to fit the inside of her locker. Include some cute magnets, a magnetic mirror, and small posters of her favorite band.

Get crafty

Stuck on you: Give your friend a handmade magnet board. Decorate a metal cookie sheet with rhinestones and jewel glue. Make a colorful background by cutting a piece of paper to fit on the cookie sheet, and attach it with double-stick tape. Decorate the sheet with pictures of you and your friend, using different-shaped magnets to hold them in place. String a long ribbon through the pre-drilled holes of the cookie sheet (or tape to the back) so that your friend can hang the board on her wall.

Friendship collage: Gather photos of the two of you together, along with images of your favorite bands from magazines, pictures of things that mean something to you both, tickets from shows you went to, or programs from recitals she was in. Paste them on construction paper or cardboard. Decorate with thoughtful words cut out from magazines. You could give her the collage as is, or consider framing it or tacking it on a small bulletin board.

Show your style: Make a logo using your own designs. Scan your artwork and bring it into a photo program on your home computer. Size the image the way you want it. Print the image onto transfer paper, following the package instructions. Ask an adult to help you iron the transfer onto a T-shirt or canvas purse to give to your friend.

Wrist warmers: Turn an old sweater into a cool cuff bracelet to give. Cut the cuff band off one shrunken wool-sweater sleeve. Cut one end of the band to create a flat strip. Measure the strip around your wrist and mark where it overlaps by 1 inch. Remove from your wrist and cut off the excess material. Sew one or two buttons along one end. Once your buttons are attached, mark on the other end of the strip where the buttons line up. Ask an adult for help cutting a small opening for each button.

Special words

Pair your gift with a thoughtful handmade card. On the inside, write a poem or story or include some quotes about friendship.

"A friend is one who walks in when others walk out."
– Walter Winchell

"A friend is one of the nicest things you can have, and one of the best."
– Anonymous

"Walking with a friend in the dark is better than walking alone in the light."
– Helen Keller

"A friend is a present you give yourself."
– Robert Louis Stevenson

Hostess Handbook

This section is your manual for throwing a party that will be fun for you and your guests. You'll find tips on pre-party prepping, deciding with your guests what activities to do, and switching gears if the party gets off track. Plus, you'll learn how to throw a fabulous party without breaking the bank and discover the best themes for boy-girl parties.

welcome!

your guide to throwing a great party

party planning

Yay! You're throwing a party. When having your own party, it's important to plan ahead. Getting details figured out in advance will help everything from setup to cleanup go smoothly.

- **When?** Certain times of the year, such as spring and holiday breaks, might be tricky since people may have other plans.
- **Where?** Will your party be at home, a nearby bowling alley, or a community pool? The location of your party can determine how many guests you can invite.
- **Who?** Talk to your parents about how many guests to invite. You might want to invite your whole class, but Mom and Dad may have other ideas. Be sure to check with them before you let the word out about your party.
- **What to do?** Write a list of ideas for activities and games you'd like to do at your party.

Checklist	
play games	✓
make crafts	✓
watch movies	✓
listen to music	✓
dance	✓
eat	✓
talk!	✓

Based on what you want to do, create a schedule of when you plan to do each activity. Just don't pack the day too full—you don't need to have every single minute planned out. Leave time for chatting.

1:00 p.m.: Guests arrive. Time for introductions and a snack.
1:30 p.m.: Pool time. Play Marco Polo and other pool games.
3:30 p.m.: Mom and Dad will make burgers and hot dogs. Time for food and chatting.
4:30 p.m.: One more game, such as charades.
5:00 p.m.: Good-byes.

Invitations

Be sure your invitation includes:

- the date and time of your party (both start and end time)
- what kind of party you're having
- the location, including the location name and address
- what guests should bring to your party
- a phone number so guests can RSVP, and the date by which you need to hear from the guests

You're invited to

Samantha's 10th Birthday Party by the Pool

Saturday, June 7 from 1 to 5 p.m.
At Samantha Johnson's House
157 Whispering Pines Lane

Bring your:

* bathing suit
* towel
* a pool toy

Please RSVP by June 1 at 310.555.1212.

too many friends

Sometimes you just can't invite every single friend to a party, because:

- Mom and Dad have set a limit on how many guests you can invite;
- the location has a limit to how many people it can hold; or
- not everyone can fit in your parents' car.

The list

When not being able to invite everyone puts you in a tough spot, create a list of all the people you'd like to invite to your party. Narrow down the choices by asking yourself which ones you're closest to or which ones you'd like to spend time with the most.

Do:
- invite friends who you know you'll have fun with
- consider which friends will have the best time together
- think about inviting someone new or someone you'd like to get to know better

Don't:
- invite people just because they're popular
- add guests to your list just because they invited you to their parties
- ask people to come to your party only to avoid hurting their feelings

Be honest

Be truthful with the people you can't invite to your party. Explain the situation. They may not be happy about it, but if you explain it clearly and honestly, they will understand.

"I wish I could invite everyone, but my parents have limited the party to just a few people. I hope you understand."

What do you do if you have a friend you don't want to invite to your party? Read what one girl did when it happened to her.

For my birthday, my parents let me invite eight friends because I was turning eight. I invited my neighbor, my family, and my good friends. There was one girl I felt I had to invite or else I knew she would get mad. But I didn't want to invite her because she can be bossy. I was also worried that she wouldn't let me talk to my other guests if she came to my party, because she wants all my attention all the time.

I decided the best thing to do was not to invite her, but she still found out about the party. I apologized to her every day for a week, but it didn't seem to help. She kept reminding me that I didn't include her and refused to forgive me. I was sorry she was angry, but I know not inviting her was the right choice. She would've been difficult and may have ended up spoiling the party.

Having a guest limit really made me think about who to invite and how everyone would get along. And, even better, I think it helped me to see who my true friends are.

Kayla, age 8

party on a budget

Parties don't have to cost much. There are plenty of ways to celebrate without spending a lot of money.

Make your own
Instead of serving store-bought cakes and snacks, make your own food for the party.

Create your own invitations
Handwrite invitations or create them on the computer. Hand deliver them rather than sending them through the mail.

Ditch the decorations
You don't have to completely change the look of a room to make it work for a party. Look for leftover streamers from past parties, or make your own decorations with things you already have. Use the back side of your science project posterboard to make a party sign. And use wrapping paper you already have to wrap empty boxes to use as centerpieces for the table. Be creative!

Play low- or no-supply games
Play games that don't require anything except items you already have around the house, such as cards or pens and paper. Turn to pages 68 and 69 for ideas.

Hold a movie party
Rent a few of your favorite movies and pop your own popcorn.

how big of a bash?

Stumped on what size party to have? Take this quick quiz!

1. You would say you're:
   a. more on the quiet side.
   b. talkative around people you know well.
   c. pretty outgoing.

2. Your ideal day would be spent:
   a. hanging out at home watching movies and relaxing.
   b. going to the beach with a friend or two.
   c. visiting your friend's day camp, where you can do new activities and meet new people.

3. What's the most important thing about a party to you?
   a. the music
   b. the people
   c. the activities

Answers

Keep it small
If you chose **more a's,** you like one-on-one interactions best. Consider having your closest pal or two over to watch movies or do something creative, such as painting, card making, or cooking.

Make it medium
If you chose **more b's,** you thrive in groups of people where you get a chance to talk to everyone. Slumber parties, skating parties, and bowling parties work best for medium-sized groups.

Go big
If you chose **more c's,** you're comfortable talking to anyone—whether you know them well or not. Plan a theme party, such as a costume party, 1950s party, or luau. Just check with Mom and Dad to make sure they're OK with your supersized guest list.

getting ready

So much to do! The clock seems to be tick-tick-ticking down to party time at warp speed! How will you get everything done before the guests arrive?

Ahead of the game

Keep stress in check by having a party plan. After you write out your guest list, take time to write out everything else you need for the party, such as:
- **Supplies:** cups, plates, silverware, napkins, and decorations
- **Things to make:** cake, cookies, invitations
- **Things to buy:** food, soda, party favors

You can also keep a party to-do schedule to keep track of what to do and when:
- **Two days before:** pick up supplies and snacks
- **Day before:** bake cake and help clean the house
- **Day of:** hang decorations, order pizza, and set up party

Ask for help

Want help hanging streamers or setting out snacks? If you need some extra hands to get ready for your party, call on your pals to lend theirs. They will likely be happy to be there for you. Plus you can do some pre-party bonding.

Your parents will need some help getting ready for the party, too. Be sure to check with them to see what they think needs to be done. Helping them out is a great—and easy—way to show how much you appreciate their letting you have a party.

Stress relief

Feeling stressed? Preparing for a party is a lot of work. Give yourself a pat on the back for all your effort, take a deep breath, and then relax and have a good time!

good times

Want to make sure everyone has a great time at your party? Take a mental walk through your party following our top five ways to become a party pro.

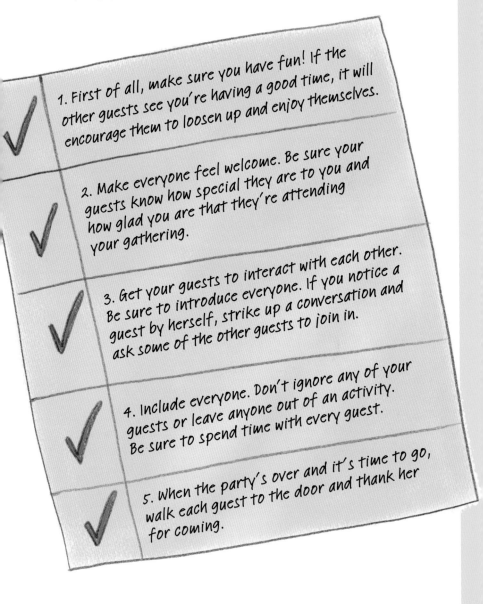

1. First of all, make sure you have fun! If the other guests see you're having a good time, it will encourage them to loosen up and enjoy themselves.

2. Make everyone feel welcome. Be sure your guests know how special they are to you and how glad you are that they're attending your gathering.

3. Get your guests to interact with each other. Be sure to introduce everyone. If you notice a guest by herself, strike up a conversation and ask some of the other guests to join in.

4. Include everyone. Don't ignore any of your guests or leave anyone out of an activity. Be sure to spend time with every guest.

5. When the party's over and it's time to go, walk each guest to the door and thank her for coming.

party play-by-play

Hi, Jennifer! Welcome to my party. Come in.

I'll put your things in my bedroom.

As your guests arrive, go to the door to greet each one individually.

Take her coat.

Courtney, this is my mom and dad, Mr. and Mrs. Gruer. Mom, Dad, this is Courtney.

Be sure to introduce each guest to your parents.

Everyone, this is Hannah Martinez.

Each time a new guest arrives, introduce her to the other guests.

Would you like some root beer or chips?

Follow me. Some of the other guests are already in the backyard.

It was so nice of you to bring a gift. We can put it over here.

...u're serving food as ...ts arrive, offer her ...ething to eat or drink.

If she brought a gift, show her where she can put it.

Lead your guest to the party location.

Just so you know, my parents' bedroom, the living room, and my brother's computer are off-limits.

First we're going to play games, then watch a movie, and finish with pizza.

...Mom and Dad will likely have ...ome party guidelines. Make sure ...ou share the rules with your guests ...nd make sure they follow them.

Let everyone know the schedule of party events.

too many choices

Having lots of party activities to choose from is a good way to keep your guests from getting bored. But if the group can't decide what to do first, it could lead to hostess headaches.

Take turns

If no one can seem to agree on what to do, the easiest way to solve the issue is to take turns.

Decide what to do based on how many people want to do it. If you're the only person who wants to do a craft and everyone else wants to dance, go along with the dancing.

If there are a few ideas being considered, do one at a time. Set a time limit for each activity, say 10 or 15 minutes. If an activity such as watching a movie requires more time, do that last.

Decisions, decisions

When you and the guests just can't seem to agree, suggest trying one of these decision makers:

Rock, paper, scissors: When it comes down to two people who can't decide, have them stand facing each other. Each one will make a fist and swing it downward three times, counting "one, two, three" at the same time. On the third count each player will throw out a hand gesture—either rock, paper, or scissors. For rock, the hand stays in a fist. For paper, the hand is spread flat. For scissors, the hand makes a sideways peace sign.

How to score: Rock crushes scissors. Paper covers rock. Scissors cut paper. The best two out of three is the winner!

rock   paper   scissors

In the bag: Write down all ideas on slips of paper. Put the slips in a bag and mix them up. Choose three slips to determine which activities to do. Or do them all, but pick slips one at a time to decide the order.

Drawing straws: Cut straws into varying lengths. Put all of them in your hand so that the tops are all at the same level. Have each guest pick a straw. Whoever gets the longest straw chooses what activity to do first.

Differing opinions

At a party or not, everyone has his or her own feelings and thoughts about things, and sometimes that can cause problems among friends. Remember that having an opinion is a good thing. Learning your friends' opinions also helps you get to know them better. But what happens when you just can't seem to agree?

• Treat the other person with respect.

• Don't make it personal. If you feel as though you must respond, keep your opinion about you. Instead of saying, "How could you like the color orange?" say what you like instead. "My favorite color is purple."

• Don't be insulting. Never say, "That's stupid!"

• Don't force your own opinion on someone else. While it's important to be heard, you don't need to be loud about it.

When your opinion stands alone

If everyone disagrees with your opinion, it can feel like you're all alone, which may be uncomfortable. Here's how to shake the awkward feeling:

• Don't take it personally. If someone doesn't agree with you, chances are she doesn't mean to be rude or mean.

• Laugh it off. Depending on the subject, you could make a joke and say something like, "Well, looks like I'm a loner on this one!"

• Let it go. Even though you may feel like a loner, no one else is probably even aware of it.

party pitfalls

Parties don't always go as planned, despite great pre-party prep. Here's what to do if a guest:

Gets homesick: Offer to let her call her parents. Often this will help ease her worries and she will be able to stay and enjoy the party. If she can't shake the blues, let her know it's OK if she needs to go home. Try to be understanding—you've probably been homesick yourself at one time or another.

Doesn't feel well: Let Mom and Dad know right away. They will be able to decide what to do.

Doesn't want to do anything you planned: Let her know that you're OK with her sitting out, but you really feel she's going to be missing out on all the fun. If she persists in being a spoilsport, continue with your party and try to let her bad attitude roll off your back. This is her problem, not yours. There's no need to get into a big argument, which would spoil everyone else's good time and could ruin your party.

Switching gears

Sometimes you might feel like your party has gotten off track. Maybe everyone's talking at once, no one seems to be interested in the activities you have planned, or guests have divided up into cliques. Sometimes you need to switch gears. Here are some ideas for jump-starting your party.

Party-staller: You're having trouble getting everyone to participate in one of your planned games.
Jump-start: Suggest a different one. Let guests vote on what they want to play.

Party-staller: Guests are sitting around not talking.
Jump-start: This is a great time to suggest a game. This will get everyone playing and talking together.

Party-staller: You put on a song you think is going to get everyone dancing, but your guests just sit there.
Jump-start: They may be shy about getting on the dance floor. Get up and dance, and call your guests up to join you. If that doesn't work, switch songs. Ask guests what songs they like to dance to.

Party-staller: The movie you rented is putting everyone to sleep. That wasn't supposed to happen!
Jump-start: Stop the movie and get up and do something to get everyone active again—dance, play a game, or get up and stretch.

Party-staller: Things have gotten out of control. Mom's favorite vase just got knocked over and people are getting way too loud.
Jump-start: You need to take control of this party—and fast. Turn off the music and call for everyone's attention. Suggest a different activity, such as eating, playing a game, or doing some other team-oriented activity. If you still can't calm things down, get Mom or Dad to help you out.

games to play

To get your party started, try a few of these fun activities that require only a few—or no—supplies.

True Story

One girl stands up and tells three stories about herself, two of which are false and one that is true. Everyone gets a chance to guess which story is true before the storyteller reveals the answer. Give each girl a chance and see who is best at bluffing.

Ice Cream Toss

Have everyone stand in front of a partner. Each person holds an ice cream cone. Each pair must place a pom-pom inside one of the cones. The game begins with players tossing the pom-poms to their partners using the cones. For every successful catch, the partners take a step backward. See which pair can go the longest—and the farthest—without dropping the pom-pom!

Monkey in the Middle

You will need lots of space to play this fun one! Girls pair up and link arms with a partner. Pairs form a large circle. Two girls do not pair up—one is the Monkey in the Middle, and the other is It. On "go," It tries to tag the Monkey. To be safe, the Monkey picks a girl to link arms with before getting tagged. Now the other girl from that pair becomes It, and the previous It becomes the Monkey in the Middle.

Team spirit

When dividing into pairs or teams for games, choose based on things that won't hurt people's feelings, such as:

- people who have birthdays in spring or summer and those who have birthdays in fall or winter
- oldest and youngest
- eye colors or hair colors
- odd or even birth date

Avoid choosing teams by closest friends or who's known each other the longest.

Celebrity Guess

On five individual strips of paper, each guest writes down one celebrity name per strip: actors, singers, politicians, writers—anyone famous that most people will know. Put all the strips into a bowl or hat. Guests are divided into two teams. Select a scorekeeper to keep track of points and choose someone to go first.

In round one, the first person chooses a name from the hat and tries to get her team to guess who it is by giving them a series of clues. The clues cannot include the name of the person. The team member gets one minute to try to get her team to guess as many celebrity names as possible. Then the next team goes.

In round two, the object is to get the teammates to guess the celebrity name by using one word only. In round three, the team members play charades to get their teammates to guess the celebrity. Whichever team has the most points by the end of round three wins.

Speed Bead

This fast and funny game is harder than it sounds! Give each player a different-colored bead. Sit in a circle. To start, someone calls out a color. The player with that color bead immediately calls out another color (no pausing and no calling your own color), and so on. When a player goofs up, everyone passes her bead to the right and gets a new color. See how fast you can go!

Time out: activities to avoid

Sidelined: Don't play games where people get tagged or voted "out." These games end up meaning that some people get to play while others don't. Pick games in which everyone can play the entire game.

Safety first: Steer clear of games where people might get hurt.

Too much information: Games that require guests to reveal personal information, such as Truth or Dare, should be avoided. Don't play any game that might hurt someone's feelings or make her uncomfortable.

Wobbly Waitress

Divide into two teams and line up.
Give each team a tray and a pile
of balloons. Set a timer for two
minutes. On "go," the first person
in each line loads the tray with
the balloons and tries to carry
them across the room to her
team's goal (a laundry basket

works fine). She must hold the tray with two hands at all times.
She dumps her balloons and goes back to give the tray to the next
person on her team, who starts with a new pile of balloons. When
time is up, the team with the most balloons in their goal wins.

Do a Dance

Girls stand in a line with their eyes covered. No one opens her
eyes until she has been tapped on the shoulder. The girl at one
end starts by opening her eyes, tapping the girl next to her,
showing her a dance move, and then covering her eyes. The sec-
ond girl taps the third girl, shows her the first dance move, adds
her own dance move, and covers her eyes again. Keep passing
the dance on until everyone has added a move. The last girl says,
"Eyes open!" and shows everyone the entire dance routine.

Have a game plan

- To avoid party boredom, make a plan.
  Don't wait until the party starts to
  think about what games to play.
  Create a schedule ahead of time and
  jot down five or six games to play,
  along with the items you'll need and
  the rules.

- If one game isn't working out—
  people are bored or just don't seem
  to get it—move on to another game
  or activity.

- Shake things up by putting friends
  on different teams. It will give them
  a chance to get to know and work
  with new people.

hostess
how-to
what you need to know about
hosting your party

the perfect party for you

What kind of party should you throw? Take our quiz to find out.

1. You would describe yourself as:
   a. sporty.
   b. creative.
   c. dramatic.
   d. thoughtful.

2. Your favorite activities are:
   a. playing outdoors with a ball in your hand and sneakers on your feet.
   b. painting, writing, cooking, or crafting.
   c. acting, telling jokes or stories, karaoke, or dancing.
   d. hanging out with your friends and getting to know them better.

3. You like parties where:
   a. there are tons of activities to keep you busy.
   b. you make things.
   c. you get to show off your outgoing personality.
   d. it's super casual, sort of like how you feel when hanging out at home.

4. Your favorite party outfit is:
   a. shorts, sneakers, and a tank top.
   b. something colorful and unique.
   c. a costume or formal dress.
   d. comfy clothes, such as jeans and a tee.

5. What's your ideal party food?
   a. healthy snacks, such as fruit and veggies
   b. homemade mac and cheese or your mom's special fudge cake
   c. something different that your guests will remember, such as sushi or fajitas
   d. traditional party treats, such as chips, pretzels, and cupcakes

6. To let off steam, you like to:
   a. play basketball or go for a walk.
   b. write a poem, draw a picture, or play some music.
   c. talk to your friends about what's going on.
   d. relax and read a good book.

Answers

Sports Star

If you chose **mostly a's,** you love playing sports and being active. Consider having your party at an ice rink or bowling alley. Or invite a few friends to see your favorite team play. If you host at home, consider activities such as basketball, soccer, or swimming (if you have a pool). If you have guests who are less athletic than you, try games such as croquet, bocce ball, or ping-pong. **Turn to page 74 for a sample sporty party idea.**

Art Smart

If you chose **mostly b's,** you're happiest when you're being creative. Plan activities that unleash your artistic side but also include everyone, such as a group craft. Or ask Mom to play chef and teach a cooking class for your guests—the best part is you can eat what you make! If you want to have the party away from home, consider going to a nearby art museum or a classic movie theater to see an old film. **Turn to page 75 for a sample artsy party idea.**

Dramarama

If you chose **mostly c's,** you love being in the spotlight. Since you love dressing up, consider having a costume party. Plan activities such as karaoke, dance contests, or even a talent show. Also consider going to a play or concert as part of your party. Just make sure you share the spotlight with the other guests. **Turn to page 76 for a sample dramarama party idea.**

Friendship Fun

If you chose **mostly d's,** you tend to enjoy time with just your closest friends instead of a big group. Your favorite parties are mellow and you prefer activities where you can really connect with other people. Slumber parties and small get-togethers are perfect for you and your guests. Play games and do activities that are all about bonding with your pals. **Turn to page 77 for a sample friendship fun party idea.**

Sporty Party

Theme: A Kickin' Party!

Invitations: Use white and black craft foam to make a flat, invitation-size soccer ball. Write the party "stats" on the back with a marker. Ask your guests to wear shirts with their favorite sports team logos, athletic shorts or pants, and sneakers.

Decorations: Make sports pennants from felt and fabric paint with sports sayings, birthday sayings, or both. Use black and white colors for things such as streamers, non-helium balloons, tablecloths, napkins, and plates.

Favors: Fill sports bottles with mini chocolate soccer balls, sports stickers, wristbands, headbands, or trading cards.

Food: Serve the kinds of food that you would find at your soccer field's concession stand: hot dogs, chips, sports drinks, and granola bars.

Activity: Even though you may be a star soccer player, your friends might not know a breakaway from a steal. Instead of holding a real soccer game at your party, try games that use soccer balls. For example, play Soccer Bowling in your yard or at a park by setting up two-liter bottles with a little sand in the bottom. Have each guest try to knock the "pins" over by kicking a soccer ball. Give each guest a point for every pin she knocks over. The guest with the most points after 3 rounds wins. Hand out fake soccer trophies, made by gluing small toy soccer balls to painted papier-mâché box tops (use a box size that works best with the toy soccer balls). Label the front of the box with stickers or paint sayings such as "#1 Kicker," "Funniest Kick," and "Good Sport."

Artsy Party
Theme: Art Studio

Invitations: Make photocopies of your art and attach it to the front of a blank card. From cardboard, cut out a frame to fit around your art card. Cover the cardboard with woodgrain scrapbooking paper. Write the party details on the inside of the card.

Decorations: Turn your living room into an art studio. Use picture frame stands to display your works of art. With each piece of artwork, include a tag with the artwork's name and a description of how it was made. For example:

> *"Sunrise" by Samantha Morris*
> *Crayon on construction paper. Samantha drew*
> *this sunrise on summer vacation at the beach.*

Favors: Hand out artist berets at the beginning of the party for the guests to wear. At the end of the party, thank them for coming by giving out paintbrushes and watercolor sets tied together with a pretty ribbon.

Food: Your guests will be busy making and creating, so instead of interrupting their creativity, keep finger foods out so that each person can help herself. Try sandwich roll-ups, mini hot dogs, and fruit covered in chocolate (try hardening chocolate syrup over strawberries and pineapple).

Activity: Create mini masterpieces. Make copies of your favorite works of art and number each one of them. Have girls pull numbers written on strips of paper from a bowl to find out which piece of artwork they get to re-create. Hand out drawing paper, pencils, colored pencils, crayons, and markers. When everyone is done, use picture-frame stands to show off their works of art.

Dramarama Party

Theme: Hooray for Hollywood!

Invitations: Fold an 8 1/2-by-11-inch piece of white paper in half lengthwise. Draw a glove shape so that the pinkie finger runs along the paper's folded edge. Cut out the white glove and glue on a fake gem for a ring. Write the party details inside the invitation. Be sure to tell the guests to dress in their best movie-star clothes!

Decorations: Go glitzy! Cover tables with a black paper tablecloth, then add gold star placemats (available at party shops). Fold black napkins accordion style and slide a ring to the center for a bowtie look. Give your front porch or entryway the red carpet effect by rolling out a red table runner.

Favors: Give such glamorous goodies as fancy sunglasses, glitzy costume jewelry, autograph books, and any silver or gold trinkets you can find!

Food: Create a theater marquee cake. Line the outside of a white sheet cake with rows of red and gold frosting. Write "A Party Starring" and your name in red icing, and decorate the cake with star sprinkles and candles. Be sure to remove the candles before eating!

Activity: You'll need several games with acting or movie-star themes. One to try is Auditions. The rules of Auditions are the same as for Simon Says, but this time the magic word is "action." One girl is the director and the rest are the actors. The director gives an instruction such as "act like a rock star." If she adds "action," girls follow the instruction. If girls do as she says when she doesn't say "action," they must strike a red carpet pose until the game is over. Ready? Action!

Friendship Fun Party
Theme: Breakfast Bash!

Invitations: Create a fried egg invitation by placing yellow card-stock circles on top of bigger, wavy-edged white shapes made from white card stock. In the yolk, write "A Breakfast Bash!" Write the party details on the back. Don't forget to ask guests to wear their PJs. (This is also a great way to end a sleepover!)

Decorations: Decorate your kitchen or dining room in a morning theme with suns and birds (use stuffed animals or look for fake birds at craft stores) and let in natural light through the windows.

Favors: Fill a favor bag with all kinds of morning gear, such as a toothbrush, toothpaste, hairbrush, barrette, muffin mix, and mini spatula.

Food: Serve breakfast foods in fun ways. For example, mix yogurt and berries together and serve the mixture in waffle cones with a spoon. Make breakfast pizzas, using English muffins as the crusts and adding toppings like hash browns, bacon pieces, sausage, and eggs. Pile doughnuts on a plate to make a breakfast cake.

Activity: Since you and your guests are super close, play The Newly Buds Game. Each player needs a partner. Send one partner from each pair into another room. Have the remaining players write their answers to all kinds of questions that you came up with before the party, such as: What color are her eyes? What's her favorite movie? Would your bud pick chocolate or vanilla? Call the players back into the room. One question at a time, the players who left the room take turns answering the questions out loud. After each answer, the player's partner reads the answer she wrote down. The team with the most matching answers wins.

your slumber party

Sleepovers are for a few good friends to spend a long night of fun together. And with that fun comes a lot of planning! Give these tips and ideas a try to keep your slumber party from being a snore.

Planning

Slumber parties are w-a-a-a-y longer than other parties. Most start around 6 p.m. and last until 10 a.m. the next morning. While some parties may work for any day of the week, slumber parties usually work best on or around the weekends.

Who's invited?

You may want to invite everyone you know, but slumber parties are best for a smaller group of girls, who

- you have the most fun with;
- you are closest to;
- make you feel good; and
- get along best with others.

Party prep

- Create a schedule of activities and get it OK'd by Mom and Dad. But don't forget to be flexible! Something you thought would take 15 minutes might take only 5 minutes. Or the game you planned on playing only once is the game your guests want to play all night. It's also a good idea to have some backup activities ready, just in case you need to fill time.

- The morning of the party, clear the space where everyone is going to sleep. Set up any decorations and put out blankets and pillows so that the space is extra cozy. Stock the area with books, magazines, and board games in case someone wants to turn in early and needs something quiet to do.

- Organize music and movies so they'll be within reach when it's time for them.

Food for thought

Planning food for a slumber party is different than for a regular party, since guests are around longer and people get hungry at different times. For dinner, plan foods that girls can help themselves to.

Sandwich station: Arrange a platter with lunch meat, cheese, lettuce, tomato slices, and bread. Don't forget the condiments, such as mayo, mustard, and pickles.

Pizza, please: Buy pre-made mini pizza crusts and let your guests be creative and pick exactly the toppings they like:

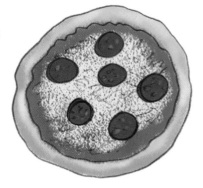

- tomato sauce
- cheese
- pepperoni or salami
- olives
- pineapple
- Canadian bacon

Grab a drink: Stock a section of the fridge with drinks and show guests where they are. Tell them to help themselves if they get thirsty.

The main meal may be over, but it doesn't mean your guests won't get the munchies later. Keep plenty of other treats on hand, such as chips, pretzels, veggies and dip, fruit, and candy.

If you're planning a night of movie watching, be sure to pop a bunch of popcorn before the party. Give each girl a bag of popcorn and set up different mix-ins to let your guests create their favorite snack mixes:

- powdered cheese
- candy
- dry ranch dressing mix
- chocolate and peanut butter chips

With the mix-ins in the bag, just seal, shake, and eat!

When guests arrive

As soon as your guests arrive, have them set up their sleeping bags in a separate room. Be sure to:

- introduce guests to your parents.
- let guests know the rules of the house.
- show guests where the bathroom is.

Break the ice

Sometimes there can be an awkward moment when everyone first arrives. Try some icebreakers to get everyone in the party mood.

Mix and match: Make copies of photos and cut them in half. Hand out one piece of paper to each guest and instruct her not to look at it. On the count of three, have all the guests look at their photo-halves and then find the guest who has the matching piece.

Guest bingo: Create a grid of 25 squares that say things like "has braces," "met a celebrity," "has a cat," "been to Hawaii," and "lived in another state." Make copies of the "bingo" card and give each guest a sheet. The goal is for the guests to find people at the party who will answer yes to the statements and sign their names on the square. The first guest to yell "Bingo!" wins.

Guess who: Before the guests arrive, write the names of different types of animals on adhesive labels. Make one for you and each of your guests. When they all arrive, line up and ask Mom or Dad to place one label on the back of each person. The goal is for each guest to figure out what animal she is by finding guests to answer her yes-or-no questions, such as, "Do I live in the forest?" Or, "Do I have long ears?"

Night owls

You're going to be up late—that's a given. But you don't want this to be the last slumber party Mom and Dad let you have. Be sure to keep the noise level down when they go to bed.

Sweet dreams

If some guests are ready to head to bed and others aren't, watching movies is a good way to keep some people entertained while others can doze off.

If the lights are out for all, remember that not everyone likes to tell scary stories at bedtime. For a funny twist, suggest that each girl tell a joke or funny story she knows instead.

Rise and shine

The best thing about a slumber party is that it's still going on when the sun comes up!

- Take turns in the bathroom so that everyone can get a chance to brush her teeth, wash her face, and brush her hair. While people are waiting, help guests gather up their things.

- For an easy breakfast, set up a bagel bar with all kinds of toppings:

  - butter
  - flavored cream cheeses
  - jams
  - peanut butter
  - honey

- When it's time to leave, walk each guest to the door to say good-bye. Thank her for coming.

- Help Mom and Dad clean up.

your boy-girl party

So you're thinking about inviting boys to your party? A boy-girl party doesn't have to be all that different from an all-girl party, as long as you're adding boys to the guest list for the right reasons:

- He's in your class and you want to know him outside of school.
- He's your neighbor, and you've known each other since before you could both walk.
- You take swimming lessons together.
- Your parents and his parents are good friends.
- He's good at history and is always nice about giving you fun ways to remember dates.
- He's nice to everyone.
- He makes you laugh.

Whatever it is, the main reason for inviting a boy should be because you are friends, OR you want to become friends.

Just like with an all-girl party, don't invite a boy just because he's popular or because he invited you to his party. Also, don't feel pressure from your girlfriends to invite boys just because they want them there. They can have their own boy-girl party for that.

A little different

The point of a boy-girl party is the same as for an all-girl party: to celebrate something and to have lots of fun. But, let's be honest, there are *some* differences—after all, there will be *boys* there!

- Conversation topics might be different. Be open to talking about different things than what you're used to talking about with your girlfriends. With the girls, you might talk about celebrities, clothing, TV shows, and even boys. With the boys, the conversations might be more about games, movies, music, and sports.

- Activities will be geared toward games for both boys and girls. For example, you might play ping-pong or go bowling instead of playing charades or doing spa treatments.

- If you watch movies together, they might not be the same ones you would watch with your girlfriends. With the girls you might watch more dramas and musical/dance films. With the boys, you might watch more action films and comedies.

Still think it would be fun to invite the boys? Great! Once you're sure, talk to your parents. Mom and Dad will likely want to know what boys you want to invite and why you want to invite them. If they're open to the idea, the next questions are "Where's the party going to be?" and "What activities will you do?" Stumped? Turn the page for some ideas!

ideas for your boy-girl party

Having boys at the party doesn't mean your party has to be completely different from all the parties you've had or been to in the past. Think about the kind of all-girl parties you've been to:

- bowling party
- pool party
- movie party
- karaoke party
- pizza party

Any of these kinds of parties would be perfect for both boys and girls, so long as the activities aren't too girly. But that doesn't mean you can't do things you like to do. You might just need to do them a little differently.

- If you like to do crafts, skip making jewelry and hair accessories and instead decorate Frisbees and sports bottles. Put out dimensional paints in all kinds of colors, and stickers with animals, flowers, sports teams, and stars on them.
- If you like to dance, play games that get your guests up and moving and require music, such as Limbo.
- If you like to dress up, throw a costume party. Have guests guess who or what each other person is dressed as for a great party icebreaker.

Try a theme party

Theme parties are great because the entertainment is all in the theme. But while a spa party might be great for you and your girlfriends, mud masks and cucumber slices aren't quite right when the boys are around. Try one of these ideas instead:

Island Party: This Hawaiian-themed party works best in the spring and summer when you can hold it outside. Serve pineapple punch, pass out leis to each guest as they arrive, and have guests make their own Hawaiian-style pizzas with cheese, pineapple, and ham.

Fiesta: Invite your friends over for a party with a Mexican twist. Serve nachos and tacos. Play *Rojo, Verde* (pronounced ROH-ho, VERR-day), a Spanish version of Red Light, Green Light. Instead of the person who is "It" saying "green light," she would say, "verde," which is Spanish for green. And for "red light," she would say "rojo," which is Spanish for red.

Mystery Party: A crime has happened in your house and it's up to your guests to investigate it. Come up with a mystery plot and create clues and maps to help your guests solve the mystery. Serve finger foods that will let your guests snack while moving from room to room, and make a cake with a large question mark on it.

Winter Wonderland: The snow and cold make a great theme for a winter *brrr*-thday. Have guests dress in their winter gear so that you can go sledding or ice skating. Have a snowman-building contest where it's girls versus boys to build the tallest snowman in 10 minutes. Serve warm foods such as chili, soup, and hot chocolate.

your parents' party

When Mom and Dad are hosting a grown-up party at your house, you become a helper.

Getting ready

Assisting your parents with party preparations will make you feel more involved in the event. You'll have a sense of pride in how well the party turns out. Plus, Mom and Dad will be really grateful for all your help. Take on tasks such as:

- setting the table
- sweeping the floor
- dusting
- hanging up decorations
- arranging flowers
- pouring chips in bowls

Good greetings

When guests arrive, make them feel welcome by greeting them at the door. If you've met them before, call them by name and tell them how nice it is to see them again. If you haven't met them before, extend your hand and introduce yourself.

Offer to take their coats and purses. Decide with your parents before the party begins where coats and purses will be kept. Be sure to let the guests know where you're taking their things in case they have to get something during the party.

When the party is over, help return items to the guests.

Refreshments

Pass out chips or crackers and let guests know where the drinks are. During the party, help clear empty plates and glasses.

Hosting the children of adult guests

Sometimes Mom's boss or Dad's friends will bring their children to your party. Because you're the closest in age to them, you may be expected to host them.

Introduce yourself and try to make them feel at home. Have Mom or Dad help you come up with a list of fun activities before the party. Consider playing a few card games, such as Uno® or Go Fish. Or do arts and crafts, such as drawing or making paper bag puppets. Set games and craft supplies out before the party so when guests arrive you don't have to go searching for stuff. Planning ahead will make you more excited about the party, and it's much easier than entertaining strangers on the fly.

Invite them to play a game, watch a movie, or listen to music with you.

If they seem a bit shy, try breaking the ice by asking a question like "What are your hobbies?" Or find out about their "favorites" by asking questions such as, "What's your favorite pizza topping?" "Who's your favorite sports star?" "What's your favorite book?" Try to ask questions that can't be answered with "yes" or "no."

Be sure to let them know the rules of the house. If they act up and break house rules, tell them. If they don't stop, let your parents know what's going on.

Don't forget to offer them a drink or snack.

Don't ignore them or leave them by themselves while you go talk on the phone or use your computer. Think about how awkward you'd feel if you were in their place.

Besides, you never know—Mom's boss's daughter might make a great new friend!

Two's company

Ask Mom or Dad if you can invite a friend to your parents' party to keep you company. She can even help out with preparations, serving, and cleanup. Just be sure she knows the rules of the house and what's expected of you during the event. And if you are supposed to host other kids, make sure the two of you don't leave the others out of your conversation or activities.

Onstage

If you play piano, sing, or dance, your parents may ask you to perform at their party. If this makes you nervous, think of it as a great opportunity to practice being onstage.

If putting on a show is your idea, make sure you ask your parents for permission before you take the stage. You don't want to surprise them with a performance they weren't expecting.

Have a friend over? Try performing a duet instead of a solo. There's always strength in numbers, and it can be a lot more fun performing with someone else. You'll share the memory and can talk and laugh about it later. Just be sure to tell your friend ahead of time—don't spring it on her at the last minute. Consider inviting her over a little early so you have time to practice.

getting gifts

opening gifts, saying thanks, and what to say when you're thinking "yuck!"

yay! presents

Gifts are fun to get, and for many people, gifts are fun to give, too. When you open presents at your party, be sure to spend a little time with each gift. Don't just rush in a mad dash from one present to the next. Take a moment or two to look each item over and really let the giver know you appreciate her thought.

- "Great poster. I love puppies!"
- "Wow, this looks like fun!"
- "Pink is my favorite color!"

Not my style
Yuck! One of your friends got you the ugliest kitten sweater known to mankind. You totally hate it—but there's no reason to hurt her feelings and tell her you do. Even if you absolutely can't stand the gift, try to say something positive about it.

"How unique."
"This is so thoughtful of you!"
"I've never seen anything like this before."

Double trouble

You might end up receiving a gift that is similar to something you already own. If this happens, thank the giver and then let Mom and Dad know after the party. Chances are, you'll be able to exchange the item for something else.

Sometimes you might even get the same gift from two different people at the same party. If this happens, laugh it off. Say:

"We know who has good taste!"
"Two's company!"
"One for my house, and one to keep at Grandma's house."

Exchange it

Gifts often come with gift receipts. Use these to return or exchange gifts that you don't like, that don't fit, or that you already have one of. Be sure to keep the receipt with the item so that you don't lose it!

Keeping track

When opening gifts, ask Mom or one of your friends to keep track of what you're getting. Have her write down what the gift is and who gave it to you. This will be really helpful when you write thank-you notes.

FROM	GIFT
Sarah	earrings
Michelle	gel pens
Loni	craft kit
Kera	puzzle book
Julie	T-shirt
Anna	PJs
Tami	travel game
Erika	purse

Clean as you go
Make sure you have a trash or recycling bag handy for dumping wrapping paper. Keep cleanup easy by tossing the paper after each gift.

Have another box on hand for any wrapping paper or bows you'd like to save. Recycling paper for other gifts or using them to make cards is good for the environment!

Gift overload
When you're done opening all your gifts, try not to feel let down that there aren't more. Take a few deep breaths and give a quick speech about how grateful you are to be surrounded by so many friends who care about you.

thanks

Writing a thank-you note for a gift within a week or so of the party is an absolute must. It's fine to say thank you in person, over the phone, or through an e-mail or text message, but those ways don't replace a handwritten note sent through the mail. It might seem like a pain, but you don't want to seem ungrateful to someone who went out of her way to do something nice for you—even if you didn't like the gift or had to exchange it. Use the gift list from the party to keep track of all the notes you need to write.

Your thank-you note
Your thank-you note should include these things:

- the date you wrote the note;
- a thank-you for the gift;
- a brief description of why you liked the gift, what reactions you've gotten about the gift, or how you've used the gift;
- something personal about the person you're writing to, such as a question about something she is interested in or a compliment about something she was wearing at the party;
- an update on how you're doing; and
- another thank-you for the gift and a thank-you if she came to your party.

End the letter by letting the person know you hope to see her again soon. Sign off with "Love," "Sincerely," or "XOXO."

As an extra party souvenir, include a group photo taken at the party.

Still need help writing a thank-you note? Use this sample letter to get ideas for what to say.

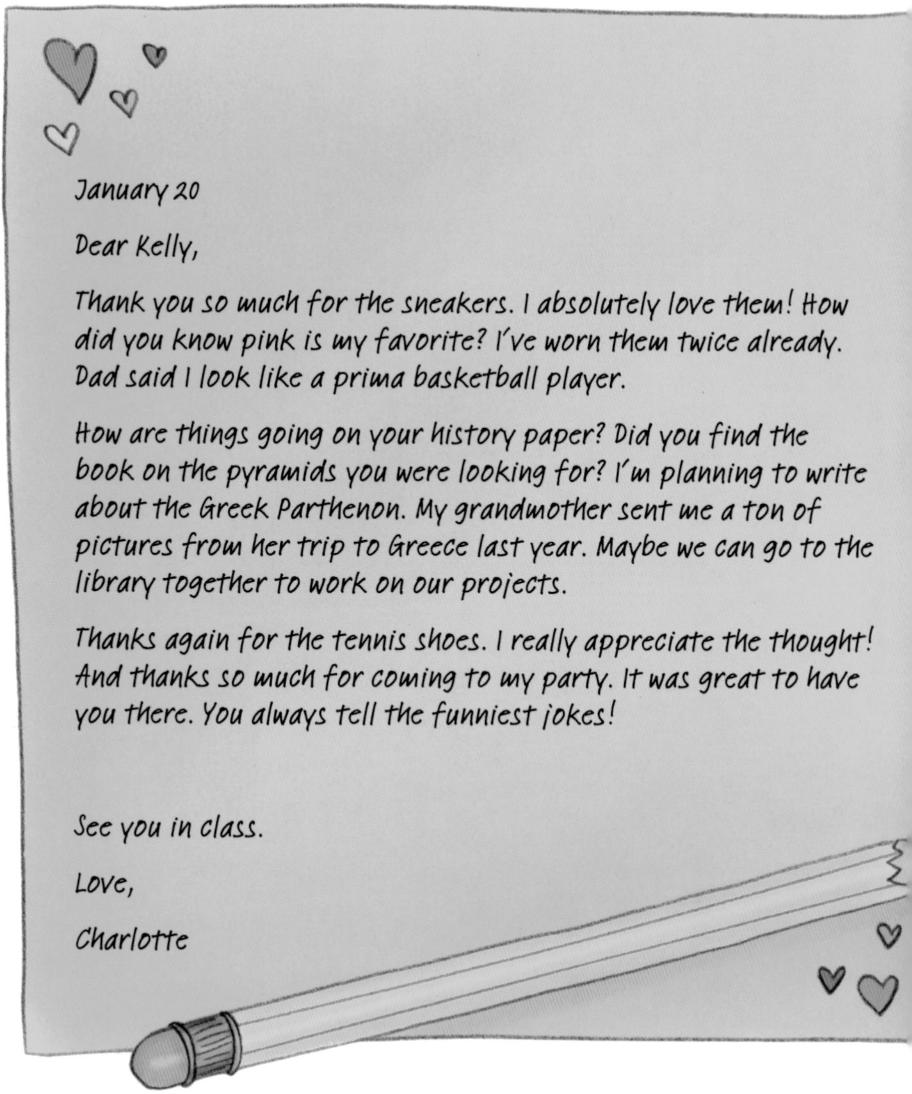

January 20

Dear Kelly,

Thank you so much for the sneakers. I absolutely love them! How did you know pink is my favorite? I've worn them twice already. Dad said I look like a prima basketball player.

How are things going on your history paper? Did you find the book on the pyramids you were looking for? I'm planning to write about the Greek Parthenon. My grandmother sent me a ton of pictures from her trip to Greece last year. Maybe we can go to the library together to work on our projects.

Thanks again for the tennis shoes. I really appreciate the thought! And thanks so much for coming to my party. It was great to have you there. You always tell the funniest jokes!

See you in class.

Love,

Charlotte

We want to hear about the parties you've been to and the parties you've thrown.

Write to:

American Girl
Parties Editor
8400 Fairway Place
Middleton, WI 53562

All comments and ideas submitted may be used by American Girl without compensation or acknowledgment.

Here are some other American Girl books you might like:

❑ I read it.

❑ I read it

❑ I read it

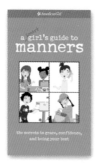

❑ I read it

❑ I read it